Stateswoman to the World

Stateswoman to the World

A Story about Eleanor Roosevelt

by Maryann N. Weidt
illustrations by Lydia M. Anderson

A Carolrhoda Creative Minds Book

Carolrhoda Books, Inc./Minneapolis

To Gladys: Keep on knitting.

Special thanks to Elizabeth Denier, of the Franklin D. Roosevelt Library at Hyde Park, New York, for her research assistance; Toni Gillman for her inspiring one-woman show, "Eleanor: A Celebration"; and Dr. Michael M. Piechowski for his psychological scholarship on the life of Eleanor.

All quotations used in this biography are from a definitive source and were reprinted with the permission of the original publishers when required.

Text copyright © 1991 by Maryann N. Weidt.
Illustrations copyright © 1991 by Carolrhoda Books, Inc.

Library of Congress Cataloging-in-Publication Data

Weidt, Maryann N.
   Stateswoman to the world: a story about Eleanor Roosevelt / by Maryann N. Weidt ; illustrations by Lydia M. Anderson.
     p.   cm. — (A Carolrhoda creative minds book)
   Includes bibliographical references.
   Summary: A biography of the First Lady, focusing on her fight for the rights of women, Blacks, and the poor, and her role as a peace advocate and delegate to the United Nations.
   ISBN 0-87614-663-9
   1. Roosevelt, Eleanor, 1884-1962—Juvenile literature. 2. Presidents—United States—Wives—Biography—Juvenile literature. [1. Roosevelt, Eleanor, 1884-1962. 2. First ladies.] I. Anderson, Lydia, ill. II. Title. III. Series.
E807.R48W4   1991
973.917′092—dc20
[B]   90-23216
[92]   CIP
                                       AC

Manufactured in the United States of America

1 2 3 4 5 6 7 8 9 10 00 99 98 97 96 95 94 93 92 91

Table of Contents

1

Grandmother Just Said No

The house was dark. The butler and the maid had shut off the gaslights and gone to bed. Six-year-old Anna Eleanor Roosevelt pressed her nose against the frosty window. Wind crept through the cracks in Grandmother Hall's old-fashioned house in New York City. Eleanor shivered. She pulled her woolen shawl close around her small shoulders.

Eleanor had sat curled up in the window seat for hours. If I look long enough and hard enough, she thought, I might spy my father. All she had seen, however, were horse-drawn carriages and street sweepers.

The fact was that Elliott Roosevelt, Eleanor's father, lived miles away in Abingdon, Virginia. He was working there, trying to prove that he could hold a steady job and stop drinking. Eleanor wrote to him often. And he wrote to her.

In his letters, Elliott called Eleanor his "Darling Little Nell" (after the character in Dickens's *The Old Curiosity Shop*). She was the star of his life. On the day of her birth, October 11, 1884, Elliott had proclaimed his daughter "a miracle from heaven."

With Elliott in Virginia, Eleanor's mother, Anna Hall Roosevelt, often took her three children—Eleanor, Hall, and Elliott, Jr.—to Grandmother Hall's house for long visits. Most of Mrs. Hall's children lived with her, even though they were in their twenties or late teens. There was Aunt Pussie, Aunt Maude, Uncle Vallie, and, when he was not touring Africa or some other continent, Uncle Eddie.

All the Hall women were strikingly beautiful, and Anna Roosevelt was no exception. Eleanor thought her mother was the prettiest woman in the world. The child would blush with excitement whenever her mother stepped into one of her shimmering satin gowns. Anna would notice

Eleanor watching her from the doorway and say, "Come in, Granny." At once, Eleanor felt ugly and clumsy. She wished the floor would open up to swallow her. One time, the little girl even overheard her mother telling her friends, "She is such a funny child, so old-fashioned."

By the fall of 1891, Anna decided that her husband was probably not coming home soon. So she bought a new house, and the family moved from the home they had shared with Elliott. Eleanor now worried that something terrible had happened to her father. Her mother and her aunts whispered about Elliott's "weakness." This made the child worry all the more.

The next fall, Anna went to the hospital for an operation. Afterward she came down with a fever, a sore throat, and a rasping cough. She had caught diphtheria. Grandmother Hall moved into the house to nurse her daughter. Eight-year-old Eleanor was sent to live with her godmother, Cousin Susie Parish. On December 7, 1892, Anna died.

Sad as she was, Eleanor was overcome with joy when she saw her father at the funeral. She was sure he had come back to take care of her and her brothers. But Anna's will was very clear. The children must live with her mother, Mary Hall.

Grandmother Hall's house was dark and often silent, despite the constant comings and goings of aunts and uncles. Grandmother Hall had spoiled her own children, and she was determined not to make that mistake with Anna's children. Grandmother hired a stern nanny and laid down strict rules. She forbade talking at mealtimes and playing games on Sundays. Every morning, each child had to take a cold sponge bath. Grandmother said it would keep them healthy.

During the first winter, Eleanor's closest brother, Elliott, Jr., caught scarlet fever. From this, he too developed diphtheria and died.

Eleanor had no playmates now, except for her brother Hall, who was just a toddler. She read for hours at a time. When she was with other children, Eleanor looked uncomfortable and felt even worse. She wore a bulky back brace to correct a bump in her spine, and her two large front teeth stuck out. Grandmother did not know much about children's fashions, so she dressed Eleanor in long black stockings and skirts that were too short. Even more awful, Grandmother made Eleanor wear flannel underwear from November to April.

No matter what Eleanor asked for, Grandmother always said no. Worst of all, she allowed Eleanor fewer and fewer outings with her father. Elliott had started drinking again, and Grandmother no longer trusted him. On the days Elliott was permitted to come for her, Eleanor would slide down one of the long, smooth banisters and land in her father's arms before he could hang up his hat. Elliott would hold her tightly, grateful for the chance to be with her.

Eleanor and Hall moved each summer with their uncles and aunts to Oak Terrace—Grandmother Hall's summer home in Tivoli, New York. This cottage on the Hudson River had fourteen bedrooms, marble fireplaces, and chandeliers with hundreds of candles. When the weather was hot (and Grandmother was not looking), Eleanor would roll down her long black stockings and wade in the river. If Grandmother caught her, she would scold, "Eleanor, ladies do not show their legs."

Once every summer, Eleanor visited her cousins at Uncle Teddy's house on Long Island. Theodore Roosevelt, Eleanor's godfather, was her father's brother. Like her father, he was witty and entertaining. He loved to gather the children around him in the gun room on the top floor. In that cozy spot, he would tell old Norse legends and recite his favorite poems.

Eleanor returned to Grandmother's town house in August of 1894, thinking more and more about her father. In two months, it would be her tenth birthday. Elliott always came toting more packages than he could carry. He had already given her a pony and two puppies (which she kept at Tivoli). What would he bring her this time?

A knock at the bedroom door tore Eleanor from her daydream. She was shocked to see both Aunt Pussie and Aunt Maude. Were they saying her father was dead? It couldn't be true. He had promised he would come back and live with her.

Grandmother Hall did not let Eleanor and her brother go to their father's funeral. She did not say why. She just said no.

Eleanor knew her father could no longer read her letters, but she still wrote to him. And she carried his letters with her. She read and reread them. Eleanor wanted to do good things so her father would be proud of her. She studied hard and did as she was told.

By the time Eleanor was twelve, she had read every book in Grandmother Hall's library. She practiced the piano and studied French and German daily. One governess taught sewing and embroidery. Another tutored her in ballet.

Mr. Dodsworth showed her how to waltz and polka.

Eleanor was invited to a dance at Uncle Teddy's when she was fourteen. All her Roosevelt cousins came, including her distant cousin Franklin Roosevelt. Sixteen-year-old Franklin asked Eleanor to dance. As they danced, Eleanor talked easily about the books she had read. The next day, Franklin told his mother, "Cousin Eleanor has a very good mind."

Eleanor spent her days waiting for the chance to be free of Grandmother Hall's control. At last, the time came. Eleanor was fifteen years old. Many well-to-do, young American women attended boarding schools in England or France. Grandmother decided that Allenswood School, near London, would be perfect for Eleanor. The headmistress was a strict Frenchwoman—with snow-white hair and piercing eyes—named Mademoiselle Marie Souvestre.

Mademoiselle "Sou" had as many rules as Grandmother Hall. Yet Eleanor adored her teacher. She loved to sit with the other girls on little chairs near the fireplace in the headmistress's library. Mlle. Sou would lecture and point to the map on the wall. She showed her students how geography affected the world's history.

One time, as a student presented a paper in front of the class, Mlle. Sou snatched it from her and tore it up. The girls sat stunned. The teacher said that she did not want her students to parrot back the same thoughts she had just given them. She demanded that the girls question information and form their own views.

Eleanor excelled in all her classes at Allenswood — except field hockey. She had never played sports. Still, Eleanor resolved to master the game. Through rain and fog, she practiced by herself for hours at a time. Her hard work paid off at last. She made the first team. Years later, she wrote, "I think that day was one of the proudest moments of my life."

Eleanor returned to America at the age of eighteen. She begged Grandmother Hall to let her continue her education. A few colleges were beginning to admit women. But once again, Grandmother said no.

② A Dutiful Wife

Instead of going to college, Eleanor did as her mother and grandmother had done. She spent a year mingling with other wealthy New Yorkers. Aunt Pussie and Aunt Maude arranged an elegant dinner dance for her. They invited all the young, single men and women from the city's richest families. Eleanor sat and watched the dancers most of the evening. Although she was tall and graceful, Eleanor did not have her mother's beauty. She felt lonely and ashamed. She left the party early.

During the rest of 1902, Eleanor attended theater parties and hosted luncheons with her Aunt Pussie. Eleanor found most of the partygoers quite dull. She longed for the many exciting conversations of Mlle. Sou and her friends at Allenswood.

At several gatherings, though, a tall, handsome

young man sought her company. He was the same fellow who had asked her to dance at Uncle Teddy's party. He reminded Eleanor of her father. He laughed and joked a lot and was always surrounded by friends. Franklin Roosevelt was studying at Harvard to be a lawyer, and he knew a great deal about politics. Eleanor liked talking to him. He was a good dancer too.

Eleanor and Franklin had many of the same friends and relatives, so they were invited to several of the same parties. They met at horse shows in Madison Square Garden and at the theater. Franklin started asking Eleanor to Harvard football games. After Uncle Teddy became president, they saw each other at the White House on New Year's Day.

Eleanor had tired of the parties and was looking for something worthwhile to do. Early in 1903, she joined a volunteer group called the Junior League. She taught dance and exercise classes to children at the Rivington Street Settlement House. A settlement house was a place where needy immigrant children could meet and play after school. Although Eleanor was not talented when it came to dancing or gymnastics, she worked to make her classes fun.

Eleanor became involved in the Consumers' League too. This was a group consisting mostly of women. They investigated working conditions in local businesses. Eleanor inspected factories where she saw four- and five-year-old children making artificial flowers until they fell over from exhaustion. In department stores, she saw clerks—usually women—who worked long shifts and were not allowed to sit down between customers. League members refused to buy goods from those businesses whose workers were treated badly.

Eleanor wanted Franklin to know about her work. She asked him to go with her to a slum apartment to visit a sick child. Franklin, who had never seen the meager living conditions of poor people, looked around and said, "Human beings can't live this way!"

In the fall of 1903, Franklin asked nineteen-year-old Eleanor to marry him. Eleanor agreed, but Franklin's mother, Sara Roosevelt, dreaded losing her only son's attention. She took Franklin on a cruise to the West Indies, hoping he might forget about Eleanor.

But Franklin returned from the ocean voyage as eager as ever to marry Eleanor. The date of the wedding, however, had to be carefully chosen.

Eleanor had asked Uncle Teddy to take her father's place at the wedding. President Roosevelt could not get away from Washington anytime he pleased. The couple picked March 17, 1905. Uncle Theodore would be in New York City then for the St. Patrick's Day parade.

Cousin Susie and her mother opened their homes for the wedding. After the ceremony, guests wished the couple well and then hurried into one of the drawing rooms to hear President Roosevelt tell stories. Eleanor and Franklin didn't feel hurt. They enjoyed Uncle Teddy's tall tales as much as everyone else.

As soon as law school was over for the year, Eleanor and Franklin sailed for Europe. Eleanor dreaded the long ocean voyage. She had never learned to swim, and she was prone to seasickness. Even so, Franklin wrote to his mother that Eleanor had not missed a meal on the way over, nor "lost any either."

The newlyweds spent the summer of 1905 honeymooning in London, Paris, Milan, and Venice. In Venice, Franklin photographed Eleanor reading a book aboard a gondola. In Paris, the couple walked hand in hand along the banks of the Seine River. They bought books and clothes and art prints at secondhand stores in tiny, picturesque villages.

On the trip home, Eleanor became ill. As soon as she got to New York, she went to the doctor to find out why she was sick every morning. She learned she was pregnant.

The couple moved their belongings into a house on East 36th Street. Franklin's mother had rented the place for them while they were gone. It was three blocks from her own New York City town house. Sara had even gone so far as to buy furniture and hire servants. Eleanor didn't like this, but she didn't say anything. She later wrote, "I was beginning to be an entirely dependent person. . . . I slipped into it with the greatest of ease."

On May 3, 1906, Eleanor gave birth to a baby girl. She named her daughter Anna Eleanor. To learn about child rearing, Eleanor read every book on the subject she could find. She discovered that babies needed fresh air. So Eleanor rigged up a boxlike contraption with wire sides. She hung it outside and put the baby in this makeshift swing for her naps. But the neighbors heard Anna crying. They called Eleanor and threatened to report her to the Society for the Prevention of Cruelty to Children. Eleanor banished her invention to the attic.

On December 23, 1907, at the age of twenty-three, Eleanor gave birth to a son. She named him James, after Franklin's father.

Eleanor soon quit her activities with the Junior League and the Consumers' League. Her mother-in-law had warned her she might bring home a disease from the slums. Eleanor did not argue.

Eleanor spent her free time knitting, embroidering, or reading. She kept up her language skills with classes in French, German, and Italian.

In the fall of 1908, the young family moved to a new home. Franklin's mother had had a double house built as a gift for her son. As before, Sara bought the furniture and hired the servants. Then she moved into the other half of the house.

This was too much for Eleanor. She felt helpless and overwhelmed by her mother-in-law's control. One evening, Franklin came home and found Eleanor sobbing. She wanted a home of her own. Franklin told her she was "quite mad."

As a mother, Eleanor never felt confident she was doing the right thing. Her strict upbringing by Grandmother Hall had not prepared her for her lively "chicks." "Playing with children was difficult for me," she said later, "because play had not been an important part of my own childhood."

The fact that Sara was always looking over her shoulder and interfering made Eleanor even more unsure of herself.

On March 18, 1909, a second son was born to the Roosevelts. Eleanor described this child as "the biggest and most beautiful of all the babies."

Despite every precaution, all three children—Anna, James, and baby Franklin—came down with the flu in the fall of 1909. The disease attacked the youngest child's heart, and he died. Eleanor blamed herself for the baby's death.

In 1910, Franklin ran in Dutchess County for the New York State Legislature. He rented a red Maxwell automobile and decorated it with American flags. He drove from town to town, talking to farmers and factory workers and anyone else who would listen.

Eleanor did not help with the campaign. She was recovering from the birth of her fourth child, Elliott. But she did hear her husband's last speech. She was not impressed. She told someone that he paused so long she was afraid he might not go on. The voters were convinced, however—enough to elect Franklin to the state senate.

On New Year's Day, 1911, the family left New York City and moved to a three-story brownstone in Albany, New York. Eleanor was twenty-six years old, and for the first time since she had married Franklin, she was out from under the eye of her mother-in-law. Years after, she wrote, "I wanted to be independent. I was beginning to realize that something within me craved to be an individual."

Eleanor felt that as the wife of a senator it was her duty to learn about politics. In the mornings, she often sat in the balcony of the capitol and listened to her husband debate state matters. The afternoons were devoted to her children. In the evenings, Eleanor played hostess to Franklin's fellow lawmakers. The Roosevelts' house was a meeting place where the arguments of the day were hashed out once again. Eleanor took part in these sessions, and they often went on late into the night. When it was time for everyone to go home, Eleanor brought out cheese, crackers, and beer. This was a signal for the guests to eat and leave.

After three years in the legislature, Franklin was chosen by President Woodrow Wilson to be Assistant Secretary of the Navy. The family moved to Washington, D.C.

War was developing in Europe by the beginning of 1914. England, France, and Russia were fighting the forces of Germany and Austria-Hungary.

America watched uneasily as the war progressed.
Eleanor's daily job was to visit and entertain other cabinet members' wives. She grew so busy she had to hire someone to help answer the mail and keep track of her appointments. Eleanor engaged a young woman named Lucy Mercer for three mornings a week. Lucy was efficient and hardworking. She came to be part of the family. Franklin called her "Lovely Lucy."

Eleanor now hurried through her social tasks so she could attend congressional hearings in which Franklin was involved. It was no longer a matter of duty. Eleanor savored the excitement of the political arena.

On an April morning in 1917, Eleanor sat in the congressional chambers with her husband. President Wilson, a peace-loving man, asked Congress to have the United States enter the war in Europe. He said, "The world must be made safe for democracy."

By the summer of 1918, President Wilson sent Franklin to Europe to report on naval operations. Eleanor stayed home to work stateside. She sent the children—Anna, twelve; James, eleven; Elliott, eight; the second Franklin, Jr., four; and John, two—to Franklin's mother's home in Hyde Park, New York. Then Eleanor got busy setting up a Navy Red Cross.

Eleanor knit woolen clothing and sewed pajamas for the soldiers. Despite hundred-degree heat, she worked twelve-hour shifts at the Red Cross canteen. Eleanor handed out coffee, sandwiches, and soup to servicemen on their way to the war. She scrubbed floors and washed dishes.

Eleanor also visited injured soldiers at St. Elizabeth's Hospital. Many of them paced their rooms or stared at the walls. Eleanor saw men chained to their beds. They mumbled to themselves. There were not enough staff people to help them. Eleanor complained to the Secretary of the Interior. Soon money was budgeted to hire more nurses and to build a recreation room.

By September, Eleanor was eager for Franklin to return home. However, instead of the happy homecoming Eleanor had imagined, Franklin arrived home on a stretcher. He was sick with pneumonia.

Eleanor made sure Franklin was resting comfortably. Then she began unpacking his suitcases. Absentmindedly, she picked up a packet of letters. She stared at them in disbelief. They were love letters from Lucy Mercer.

Eleanor marched into Franklin's bedroom waving the letters. Franklin admitted he had been having a love affair with Lucy. Eleanor felt betrayed.

She had tried to please her husband, to make his interests her own. It seemed that somehow she had failed. She offered Franklin a divorce.

When Franklin's mother heard what was happening, she told Franklin she would cut him out of her will if he divorced Eleanor. Political advisers told Franklin that his career in politics would be ruined by a divorce. Franklin vowed that he would never see Lucy again. So Eleanor decided to remain with him for the children's sake. But Eleanor's confidence in herself was crushed.

On November 11, 1918, the war ended. People all over the world rejoiced. For centuries-old cities in Europe, it was a time of rebuilding. For thirty-four-year-old Eleanor, it was time to put together the pieces of her life.

Eleanor joined Franklin as he toured Europe after the war. She saw the ruins of cathedrals and entire villages that had been destroyed. Her own sorrows seemed light compared to the suffering she witnessed.

③

The Campaign Trail

In June of 1920, Eleanor was with the children at the family's vacation cabin on Campobello, a Canadian island off the coast of Maine. A telegram arrived. It said that the Democratic Convention in San Francisco had nominated Franklin for vice president of the United States. Eleanor was glad for her husband. But she didn't care much about it for herself. Later she wrote, "It never occurred to me to be much excited."

Eleanor and Franklin set out on a four-week campaign trip through the Midwest, traveling as far west as Colorado. Their train, called the Westboro, stopped at stations along the way. Franklin gave speeches from the platform in the back of their car. The schedule was rough, but Eleanor enjoyed the trip. She was thrilled to see parts of the United States she had never seen.

Franklin's friend and adviser Louis Howe came along. Eleanor had never liked the little man with the rumpled clothes and the continual cigarette in his hand. But Louis was fond of Eleanor. He resolved to try winning her friendship. First he asked for her advice on speeches he had written for Franklin. Then he discussed campaign tactics with her. Gradually Eleanor began to trust Louis's judgment. Soon the two were close friends.

Despite vigorous campaigning, Franklin and his presidential running mate, James Cox, were defeated. The Roosevelts moved from Washington, D.C., back to the house in New York City. Franklin became a partner in the law firm of Emmet, Marvin & Roosevelt.

Eleanor, having tasted politics, wanted more. She became a board member of the New York State League of Women Voters. In 1920, she attended her first state and national league conventions. She also spoke in public for the first time. Because she was afraid, she giggled. Louis Howe heard her and offered to coach her in public speaking. He gave her this advice: "Have something to say, say it, and then sit down."

In January of 1921, Eleanor became chairperson of the league's legislative committee.

With the help of Elizabeth Read, a New York lawyer, Eleanor checked on laws concerning women. Then she reported her findings to the league's members.

The summer of 1921 was to have been a time of relaxation for the Roosevelts. The entire family stayed on Campobello Island. They fished and sailed. Friends came to visit.

In early August, Franklin began complaining that he felt sluggish. One afternoon, as the family sailed home, they stopped to help fight a forest fire. They arrived home around four o'clock.

Tired, Franklin thought a good swim might perk him up. The children agreed, and they all clambered off for a dip. After two long swims and a run home, Franklin sat in his bathing suit and looked through the mail. He felt chilled and said he was too tired to eat supper. He dried off and crawled into bed to warm up.

The next day, Franklin was running a fever and could barely move his legs. Eleanor slept on a cot in his room in case he needed anything. Franklin was in severe pain. After several days, he could move his arms, back, and hands only slightly. He couldn't hold a pen. A specialist diagnosed Franklin's disease as infantile paralysis, or polio.

By the end of September, the doctors thought Franklin was strong enough to be moved. Eleanor arranged for a private railroad car to transport her husband home.

Eleanor settled Franklin into a third-floor bedroom in the packed house in New York City. Franklin's nurse and Louis Howe moved into the third floor too, so they could help Franklin easily. The Roosevelt children were stuffed into the rest of the bedrooms, which were on the fourth floors of the double house. After all the rearranging, Eleanor was left with no room of her own. She slept in one of the younger boys' rooms and dressed in her husband's bathroom. Looking back on this time, Eleanor wrote, "In many ways this was the most trying winter of my entire life."

Eleanor came toe to toe with her mother-in-law over Franklin's illness. Sara thought her son should retire to her home in Hyde Park and remain there as an invalid for the rest of his life. Eleanor believed that Franklin should exercise his weakened muscles and return to his former activities.

With Louis's encouragement, Eleanor stood up to her mother-in-law and won. Franklin did walk again. His political career was far from over.

On the Banks of Val-Kill

Eleanor's career in politics had just begun. Louis Howe urged her to expand her activities in the Democratic party. In the spring of 1922, Eleanor met Marion Dickerman and Nancy Cook. Both women were active in the Women's Division of the Democratic State Committee.

Eleanor joined Marion and Nancy in editing the *Women's Democratic News.* Louis Howe taught Eleanor how to prepare the "dummy" of the paper for the printer, how to write headlines, and how to attract advertisers. To speed up her work, she learned typing and shorthand.

Eleanor also worked to raise money for the Women's Division, organized petition campaigns, and lobbied the legislature to pass important laws.

The laws that concerned Eleanor most were those dealing with women and children.

Eleanor's courage expanded with each new interest. She had once been undecided as to whether or not women should have the right to vote. But by 1923, after three years of having this right, Eleanor urged members of the League of Women Voters to inform themselves on issues and vote intelligently.

At the New York State Democratic Convention in 1924, Eleanor led the female Democrats in a successful revolt for their rights. The men wanted to choose the female delegates. Eleanor said that the women should pick their own representatives. She held her ground, and the women finally won.

More and more, Eleanor depended on friendships with the women in her life. In the fall of 1924, Eleanor invited Nancy and Marion to Franklin's mother's estate for a picnic on the banks of Val-Kill Stream. Franklin and the youngest boys—Franklin, Jr., ten, and John, eight—joined them. Eleanor sighed that this would be their last weekend at Hyde Park for the season. Franklin suggested that Eleanor and her friends build a year-round cottage near the stream. He offered them the land, and they readily accepted.

All through the winter of 1924 and into the next spring, Eleanor, Nancy, and Marion worked on the design of their cottage. Eleanor used some money of her own to build it. The stone house came to be called Val-Kill Cottage. *Val-Kill* means valley stream in Dutch. In June, Eleanor once again picnicked with her friends at Hyde Park. While the children played, the women thought of a plan. Why not start a business at Val-Kill? They could employ the men and women from nearby farms who needed work in the winter.

Thus began the idea for Val-Kill Industries. Nancy Cook had once taught woodworking. She volunteered to design early-American-style furniture and teach workers how to build the pieces. Eleanor was to be in charge of selling the items.

By New Year's Day of 1926, Val-Kill Cottage was completed enough for a housewarming party. The entire Roosevelt family was on hand, and everyone, including Sara Roosevelt, sat down to dinner using nail kegs for chairs. Later, of course, Val-Kill Industries provided the cottage's beds, tables, chests, and chairs.

Eleanor, Marion, and Nancy started another project in 1927. They bought Todhunter School, a private girls' school in New York City. Marion became the principal. After her son John went away to school, Eleanor became vice principal. She also taught English and American literature, American history, and current events three days a week. Her current events course was called *Happenings.* She assigned readings from popular magazines and held informal discussions. She took the girls, via subway, to visit poor neighborhoods, police lineups, court sessions, and street markets.

Mlle. Souvestre had taught Eleanor to use her mind. Now Eleanor was showing her pupils how to do the same. Eleanor told reporter Lorena Hickok, "I've liked teaching more than anything else I've ever done."

While Eleanor worked on Val-Kill Industries and Todhunter School, Franklin worked on building up his strength. He had regained some use of his arms and legs. Swimming in the hot springs at Warm Springs, Georgia, had helped him recover. So he bought an old resort there and had it made into a top-notch therapy center for polio victims.

In 1928, politics returned as a major priority in the Roosevelt household. Franklin nominated New York Governor Al Smith for president at the Democratic National Convention. Smith, in turn, suggested that he campaign for the governorship.

Franklin took up the challenge.

Eleanor supported him, of course, but she was more interested in campaigning for Al Smith. Besides, she was beginning to have a life of her own. She was not pleased at the thought of being the wife of an elected official again.

When the 1928 elections were over, Eleanor had good reason to be upset. Smith had lost, and her husband had won. After the election, she told a reporter for the *New York Evening Post,* "If the rest of the ticket didn't get in, what does it matter? . . . No, I am not excited about my husband's election. I don't care. What difference can it make to me?"

For better or worse, the move to the Governor's Mansion in Albany in 1929 did make a difference in Eleanor's life. Reluctantly, she had to resign from the Women's Division of the Democratic State Committee. She did, however, continue editing the committee's newspaper. And she kept teaching three days a week at Todhunter School.

Eleanor took on new responsibilities as wife of the governor. One of Franklin's jobs was to make inspection tours of the state's prisons, mental institutions, and hospitals. He asked that Eleanor come along to serve as his eyes as well as his legs.

The couple found that they made a good team. While Franklin chatted with the press, Eleanor conducted the real investigation. She lifted lids and peered into pots on the stove. She opened drawers and looked through linen closets to make sure they were clean. It soon became such a habit that sometimes when visiting her friends, she would pull open a drawer or peek into a medicine cabinet.

Throughout New York State and the United States, life was hard for most people. Nineteen twenty-nine was in the time of the Great Economic Depression. Many people had lost money through stock-market investments. Men, women, and children roamed the streets without homes and jobs. On occasion, people would approach Eleanor on the street and ask for money or food. She would hand them a card with her address on it. The card was an invitation for them to be her guests for dinner.

In 1930, Franklin ran for a second two-year term as governor. This time, Eleanor told a reporter for the *Evening World,* "If my husband is reelected, I shall be pleased. And if he isn't—well, the world is full of interesting things to do."

No Ordinary First Lady

The people of New York elected Franklin again. By this time, Anna was married and James was a student at Harvard. Elliott, Franklin, Jr., and John were at Groton, the boarding school their father had attended.

When Franklin's second term as governor neared an end, Franklin ran for president of the United States. On November 8, 1932, the family waited for election results at Franklin's mother's home in Hyde Park. A telegram arrived at midnight. Franklin had won. Realizing that no one had eaten dinner, Eleanor went to the kitchen, put a couple of frying pans on the stove, and began cracking eggs. Soon she was scrambling eggs for newspaper reporters, friends of the family, and complete strangers who dropped by to offer their congratulations.

Franklin was sworn in as the 32nd president of the United States on March 4, 1933. After the festivities, Eleanor supervised as her family's belongings were moved into the White House. The movers were not going fast enough for Eleanor, so she carried some things herself. She was not a typical First Lady. In fact, she told the reporter Lorena Hickok, who was now her close friend, "There isn't going to be any First Lady. There is just going to be plain, ordinary Mrs. Roosevelt."

True to her word, Eleanor tried to keep the atmosphere at the White House informal. Grandchildren ran up and down the stairs, and played on the elevators. More than once, Eleanor shocked her guests by greeting them at the White House door. Though there were plenty of servants, plain, ordinary Mrs. Roosevelt liked to do things herself.

Eleanor was usually in too much of a hurry to wait for attendants to help her. Yet she quickly saw where she could help them. The servants lived in the basement, which was damp and gloomy. Eleanor hired workers to decorate and remodel this area of the White House.

Eleanor's own living quarters consisted of a large two-room suite on the second floor of the White House. Her writing desk stood near a tall window.

Outside the window was a magnolia tree that President Andrew Jackson had planted. Many evenings, Eleanor sat at her desk until well after midnight. She answered some of the more than 30,000 letters a month she received.

In the White House, Eleanor and Franklin's working relationship grew stronger. Eleanor communicated with her husband daily—either in person or in writing—about private and public issues. Eleanor often pushed for change, while Franklin was inclined to hold back. Through Eleanor's prodding, Franklin employed women in top government positions. Franklin agreed to Eleanor's suggestion that he appoint Frances Perkins as the Secretary of Labor. This was the first time a woman served in a presidential cabinet post. Franklin also named Nellie Ross as Director of the Mint and Florence Allen as the first female judge on the United States Court of Appeals.

To help female newspaper reporters, Eleanor held "women only" press conferences. The first one took place on March 6, 1933, in the Red Room of the White House. Eleanor had two purposes in mind. One was to encourage publishers to hire female reporters. The other was to keep women informed on subjects of interest to them.

Eleanor discussed such topics as child labor, nutrition, and women's roles in society. She steered away from questions concerning clothing and hairstyles.

Only one man ever attended Eleanor's press conferences. King George VI of England and his wife, Queen Elizabeth, were visiting. Eleanor invited the queen to sit in on the conference. When no one was looking, King George walked in and started shaking hands with the reporters. No one, of course, dared ask the king of England to leave.

Eleanor's days as First Lady were full. She saw streams of people each day. Some came to seek her advice. Others wanted money for various projects. Eleanor considered herself a public servant, whose duty was to speak with anyone who asked to see her.

Eleanor wrote to her friend Lorena Hickok describing her days. Lorena thought the letters were so interesting that she suggested Eleanor write a newspaper column. In 1935, at the age of fifty-one, Eleanor wrote the first "My Day" column. Her earliest columns centered on family life and health. As time went on, Eleanor explored more serious social concerns in her writing, such as poverty, racism, and unemployment.

She also wrote a full-length article every month on one of her interests for a magazine called the *Woman's Home Companion.*

Proud of her status as a journalist, Eleanor joined the American Newspaper Guild. She wrote her "My Day" column every day, no matter where she was. Sometimes she dictated the column to her secretary while holding a grandchild on her lap. Once when Eleanor had a fever of over one hundred degrees, Franklin offered to write the article for her. Eleanor refused to let him. She said later that she was afraid that Franklin would take it over, and she'd lose her job.

Eleanor thought women should be paid for the work they did. Not only that, but women should be paid well—even if one were the wife of a president. Eleanor delivered a series of radio broadcasts. For one series, she was paid five-hundred dollars a minute. Eleanor donated the money to the American Friends Service Committee to aid unemployed miners in West Virginia.

In February of 1939, Eleanor publicly addressed the problem of racial prejudice. The Daughters of the American Revolution had scheduled black singer Marian Anderson to perform for them at Constitution Hall, in Washington, D.C.

Some DAR members, however, canceled the invitation. They said that since black people were not allowed to enter Constitution Hall, Marian should not be allowed to sing there. Eleanor was angry. She announced her resignation from the DAR in her column. Then she helped arrange a new concert in front of the Lincoln Memorial on April 9, Easter Sunday. Nearly 75,000 people came to hear Marian Anderson sing.

Later that year, Eleanor attended the Southern Conference on Human Welfare in Birmingham, Alabama. When she arrived, she found that one side of the room was for white delegates, the other for black. Eleanor placed her chair in the aisle between the two sections. She did not make a speech—yet everyone knew what she was saying.

Eleanor's efforts to have all people treated with respect were only beginning. When the president of the National Indian Association spoke out against Native Americans keeping their customs, Eleanor resigned as honorary chairwoman. She supported Indian schools. She also aided migratory Hispanic workers and Appalachian communities. During World War II, Eleanor argued with Franklin about sending Japanese Americans to camps, and she fought for aid for Jewish refugees.

World War II began in the fall of 1939, when Adolf Hitler stormed Europe. His German troops invaded Poland, Norway, Denmark, Belgium, France, Luxembourg, and the Netherlands. Britain prepared to be next. Two of Germany's supporters were Italy and Japan. Italy had invaded Northern Africa, and Japan had attacked China and Southeast Asia. Most Americans wanted to stay out of these wars. Franklin, however, urged Congress to give Britain, France, and the Soviet Union all aid possible "short of war." The United States also stood behind China and stopped trading with Japan.

Franklin ran for a third term as president in 1940. His party did not give him an easy victory. Many Democratic delegates were upset about Franklin's choice for vice president—Henry Wallace. Frances Perkins stepped in. She telephoned Eleanor at Val-Kill and asked her to fly to Chicago to speak to the convention.

Eleanor walked into a convention hall that was thick with cigar smoke. Everyone was shouting at everyone else. Those who weren't shouting were booing. Eleanor stepped to the podium. She spoke in a calm, deliberate voice. She told the delegates to rise above their personal motives.

"This is a time when it is the United States we fight for," she said. "No man who is a candidate or who is president can carry this situation alone. This is only carried by a united people who love their country."

Eleanor said what she had to say. Then she sat down. As she took her seat, the organist played "God Bless America." The delegates confirmed the nomination of Henry Wallace, and the convention went on without further delay.

Eleanor had spoken out against war for many years. Shortly after Franklin was elected for his third term, Eleanor addressed the Illinois League of Women Voters. She told the women that their most important task was to work for the prevention of war.

On December 7, 1941, Japan attacked American troops in Pearl Harbor, Hawaii. The United States immediately declared war on Japan and later on Germany. This meant that Eleanor became deeply involved in World War II, not only as a representative of the government, but also as a mother. All four of her sons served the country in the armed forces.

Eleanor put on her Red Cross uniform once more. She gave blood, knitted socks for soldiers, and sold war bonds. She slogged through mud in the rain to visit American servicemen in England. She toured parts of London that had been demolished by bombs.

In 1943, Eleanor took off on a five-week trip to visit wounded soldiers in the South Pacific. She talked with every soldier in every hospital—some 400,000 men. She bounced along rough roads in army jeeps and trucks. Once Eleanor even typed her "My Day" column with half-frozen fingers, riding in the bomb bay of a plane on the way to Guadalcanal.

Eleanor was one of the most globe-trotting First Ladies in history. She covered thousands of miles a year. She put on overalls and went into the coal mines to talk to miners in Pennsylvania, West Virginia, and Ohio. Wearing boots, she trudged through cornfields in the Midwest. Admiral Byrd, the explorer, joked that in his hut near the South Pole, he always set an extra place at supper—just in case Eleanor decided to drop in.

Many people criticized Eleanor for her traveling. One man wrote to her, "Why don't you buy yourself some stuff to knit with, instead of using the army's gas for your trips?" Little did he know that Eleanor usually knitted while she traveled.

Nineteen forty-four was an election year. Eleanor dreaded another campaign. Franklin was not as "peppy" as usual, and she worried about him. A heart specialist had diagnosed Franklin as having "congestive heart failure." For her part, she was tired of being in the public eye. Before the election, she told a friend, "I wish I were free."

6

To Do Something Useful

Franklin was elected to a fourth term as president in 1944. With British Prime Minister Winston Churchill and Soviet Premier Joseph Stalin, he worked to bring an end to World War II. The long meetings and extensive traveling exhausted him.

On the morning of April 12, 1945, Eleanor held her usual "women only" press conference. She did not know it would be her last. That afternoon, she was called out of a meeting to learn that Franklin had died. He had been resting in Warm Springs, Georgia, when he collapsed.

Eleanor told her friends that she would miss Franklin "intellectually." He had been her husband, friend, and partner for forty years. She had relied on his advice in many situations—as he had counted on hers. Despite his betrayal, Franklin had been a great support in her life.

Eleanor was controlled and dignified throughout Franklin's funeral. Her main concern was that things be done as he would have wished. Any sadness she felt was hidden from public view.

The United States mourned its beloved leader, and Vice President Harry Truman was sworn in as president. Truman offered Eleanor his condolences and asked what he could do for her. Knowing the troubles he would face as president, she replied, "Oh, no, what can we do for you?"

Eleanor moved out of the White House and into the cottage at Val-Kill. She felt at home there. When weather permitted, Eleanor would spend the night sleeping on the porch. She would wake to watch the sun come up over the birch trees that surrounded Val-Kill Stream and Pond.

Each morning, Eleanor rose early, walked the dogs, and started answering the mail. She still received about a thousand letters a week. Most days, she invited guests for lunch. The guests might include one or two of her children or grandchildren, a visiting dignitary, some Mormon missionaries who were in the neighborhood, or someone she met on the train.

Residents of nearby Hyde Park became used to seeing Eleanor standing in grocery checkout lines.

She often walked her two Scottie dogs, Fala and Tamas McFala, along roads and through fields. Eleanor moved at such a pace that the dogs had to run to keep up with her.

The grounds of Val-Kill became the site of the annual outing for the boys of Wiltwyck School. Wiltwyck was a center for delinquent boys. Eleanor would hand out hot dogs and dish up potato salad. When the boys were well fed, Eleanor would choose a shady spot on the lawn and read to them. She always read from books by Rudyard Kipling. The *Just So Stories* was her favorite.

Some months after Eleanor left the White House, President Truman brought her back into political service. He needed a delegate to the United Nations. So he appointed Eleanor. She was sixty-one-years old and the only woman in the United States delegation.

The United Nations Assembly met for the first time on January 10, 1945, in London. One issue of immediate concern to the United Nations—and to Eleanor personally—was the thousands of European refugees left homeless by the war. Many were children. Eleanor worked with the United Nations International Children's Emergency Fund (UNICEF) to find homes for the youngsters.

She gave her own money to support twenty of the children. Through her UNICEF work, Eleanor gained the title "Friend of the World's Children."

In 1946, Eleanor became head of the United Nations Commission on Human Rights. The purpose of the commission was to draft a worldwide statement on civil rights. It seemed a simple enough task. But the delegates fought long and hard over every word.

The Universal Declaration of Human Rights was finally approved by the United Nations in 1948. The delegates rewarded Eleanor with a standing ovation. She responded by inviting them all to Val-Kill for a picnic.

By this time in her life, Eleanor had earned the love and respect of the American people. When the February 1948 issue of the *Woman's Home Companion* polled its readers (over three million) to name their favorite American, men and women alike chose Eleanor Roosevelt. People around the world admired her as well. The *London Daily Herald* wrote of her, "She is . . . a worker for all just causes, a woman who would have won fame had she never married a famous man."

In 1952, at the age of sixty-eight, Eleanor was formally invited to India by Prime Minister Nehru.

On the way there, she called on the heads of government in Lebanon, Syria, Jordan, and Pakistan. In Pakistan, Eleanor was invited to a purdah party, which is for women only. Eleanor loved it. The women danced and taught Eleanor their native songs. She showed them how to square dance to Pakistani music.

In Bombay, India, Eleanor appeared at a reception in her honor wearing a linen dress and tennis shoes. (She had had no time to change her clothes, and she had thought it would be rude to be late.) With her hands folded, she bowed her head in a traditional Indian greeting. The crowd cheered, "Eleanor Roosevelt zindabad!" (Long live Eleanor Roosevelt!) After this trip, she wrote a book entitled *India and the Awakening East.* No one knew when she had found time to write it.

When President Eisenhower took office in 1953, he did not reappoint Eleanor to the United Nations. But the world was still "full of interesting things to do." She traveled to Japan, where she met with Emperor Hirohito and his wife, the Empress Nagako. Eleanor talked about how women around the world were beginning to free themselves from the tradition of slavery. The empress listened intensely. They talked for over an hour.

Eleanor would not leave Japan without visiting Hiroshima. Hiroshima was the first city to have been hit by a nuclear weapon. It had happened at the end of World War II, while Truman was commander in chief of the army. Saddened at the extreme suffering she saw, Eleanor said, "God grant to men greater wisdom in the future."

Once at home again, Eleanor volunteered at the American Association for the United Nations. She wanted to build support among the American people for the UN. She journeyed from one end of the United States to the other. Through her efforts, more than two hundred local AAUN chapters were formed.

Eleanor celebrated her seventieth birthday in October of 1954. Several friends surprised her with a lavish party at the Hotel Roosevelt in New York City. Many important politicians and dignitaries attended. But for Eleanor, the special guests of the evening were the boys from Wiltwyck School. They sang her favorite song, "Beautiful Dreamer," and presented her with one hundred pot holders—each handmade by one of the boys. Eleanor kept every one.

Eleanor's public career was not finished yet. In 1957, Eleanor traveled to the Soviet Union.

There she interviewed Premier Nikita Khrushchev for the *New York Post*. Eleanor was not shy in the questions she asked. She challenged Khrushchev on his country's treatment of its Jewish citizens.

When Khrushchev toured the United States, Eleanor invited him to tea. Some people criticized her, calling her a Communist. She responded, "How, I wonder, do these people feel that we can learn to live together—as we must—if we cannot sit down over a cup of tea and quietly discuss our differences?"

John F. Kennedy became president in 1961, and he reappointed Eleanor to the United Nations. When she arrived to take her seat, the delegates gave her another standing ovation.

Kennedy also asked Eleanor to chair the National Commission on the Status of Women. Eleanor was delighted. In August of 1962, she delivered a progress report to the president. One of the goals she outlined was a federal law granting equal pay to women and men.

Eleanor had once used radio to air her views. Now in the 1960s, she hosted a television show called "Prospects of Mankind." On it, she interviewed important people in the news. Even President Kennedy was a guest on the show.

Eleanor believed the future of the world was in the hands of young people. She felt strongly that children needed to learn about different cultures. "The world is smaller than you think," she often told her audiences.

A record company asked Eleanor to be part of a concert recording for children called *Hello World!* The concert took listeners on a musical tour of various countries. Eleanor was the tour guide.

On November 7, 1962, Eleanor Roosevelt died at the age of seventy-eight with her children at her bedside. People all over the world mourned. Many praised how much Eleanor had accomplished in her life. As for Eleanor herself, she had once summed up her ambitions in an article for *Success* magazine. What she most wanted out of life, she wrote, was "the opportunity for doing something useful, for in no other way... can true happiness be attained."

Bibliography

Davis, Kenneth. *Invincible Summer.* New York: Atheneum, 1974.
———. "Miss Eleanor Roosevelt." *American Heritage,* October 1971, 49-59.

Flemion, Jess, and Colleen M. O'Connor, eds. *Eleanor Roosevelt: An American Journey.* San Diego: San Diego State University Press, 1987.

Hickok, Lorena. *Eleanor Roosevelt: Reluctant First Lady.* New York: Dodd, Mead & Co., 1962.

Jacobs, William. *Eleanor Roosevelt: A Life of Happiness and Tears.* New York: Coward-McCann, 1983.

Lash, Joseph. *A Centenary Portrait of Eleanor Roosevelt.* New York: W. W. Norton & Co., 1984.
———. *Eleanor and Franklin.* New York: W. W. Norton & Co., 1971.

Roosevelt, Eleanor. *The Autobiography of Eleanor Roosevelt.* New York: Harper, 1961.
———. *This is My Story.* New York: Harper, 1937.
———. *You Learn by Living.* Philadelphia: Westminster Press, 1960.

Roosevelt, Elliott. *Eleanor Roosevelt, With Love: A Centenary Remembrance.* New York: E. P. Dutton, 1984.

Scharf, Lois. *Eleanor Roosevelt: First Lady of American Liberalism.* Boston: Twayne, 1987.

Youngs, J. William T. *Eleanor Roosevelt: A Personal and Public Life.* Boston: Little, Brown & Company, 1985.